D1534907

Mirrors On Uncertain Mornings

To Brian,

with gratitude,

19 April 2007

MIRRORS ON
UNCERTAIN MORNINGS

Grant Johnston

Talonbooks   Vancouver   1988

copyright © 1988 Grant Johnston

published with the assistance of the Canada Council

Talonbooks
201/1019 East Cordova Street
Vancouver, British Columbia
Canada V6A 1M8

This book was typeset in Goudy and Caslon by Pièce de Résistance Ltée., and printed by Hignell Printing Ltd.

Printed in Canada

First printing: September 1988

The author wishes to express his appreciation to the Canada Council whose support bought him the time to let some of these poems germinate. Some of these poems were published in earlier versions in *A Compass of Open Veins*, new press, 1970.

Canadian Cataloguing in Publication Data
Johnston, Grant, 1941-
   Mirrors on uncertain mornings

Poems.
ISBN 0-88922-259-2

I. Title
PS8569.045M5 1988   C811'.54   C88-091487-4
PR9199.3.J64M5 1988

Contents

I dedicate this book with love and gratitude to my wife Patsy.

Letters

in letters
i can write intimate things
how i miss your small gestures
which speak more than words
that i would rather be
with you than me

yet when we're together
at the point of ecstasy
i see your face shifting
i shift to other faces
   to hold a vision
i strike a match

in letters i don't strike matches
i butt cigarettes
i mail words across
a great distance

Fisherman

for Everet Crouse

the river's low and salmon few
   stooped and arm-weary
endlessly he casts endlessly
while it numbs him through
and through new waders green
on bottom slime

down river heading seaward
he casts tide in on pools
he doesn't know

when he's through
what do rivers
wordless
do

Insomnia

i've fixed
the bathroom leak
   the seconds continue
to drip one
by one

Town Crier

you may have seen him
  late afternoons he's a regular
at the same corner riding
an early happy hour
wearing a carnival stetson
and loud incoherent
words

in one hand's a shopping bag
  the other's jerking like a toy soldier
points directions to everyone
and no one
in particular

passersby step around him
like a puddle its size
determined by the degree
of their discomfort

i've boarded a bus with him
he was quiet   got off
somewhere

you see him
in other places
like shop windows   murky puddles
and mirrors on uncertain
mornings

Summer Storm

wind tugs at the house   ripples
the long grass down to the shore
    sprouting sails
i take up my pen
    brash as a foghorn
i begin to steer
and on my gimpy leg
a jig i do
on the sole deck there is
on such a voyage

The Loft

often at night
i leave the red door
open to my loft
knowing the wind will rattle it
hoping the wind
is you

and though you never climb the stairs
if i get up and close the door the wind
caresses   the wind
leaves

Souvent le soir

quand dans le soir qui tombe
je laisse ouverte ma porte
ma porte sur le soir
je caresse l'espoir
que le vent qui la fait battre
ne soit nulle autre que toi

et quand je ferme la porte
ma porte sur le soir
même si ce n'est pas toi
le vent léger du soir
caresse mon visage
et me laisse dans le noir

The Ceremony of Snow

the blind altar
the mouth
of a gradual windowsill
which begs only
at night
while outside the city
on telegraph wires
slow music swirls
elegant and dark

Dancer

for Patsy

as day comes and goes
so do you naked beneath the sun
weave in and out of light
   your breasts swung fruit
in season before fall
   the white stretch marks
of your thighs dance
are rivers too
   blest am i to be
all present
before all

Charlie Craig: In Memoriam

an old bachelor
dying in hospital

visitors

outside his door
a woman hesitates

40 years since then
and the silence in between

completes a necklace
of slow pearls

you were alone   we together
  babbling to yourself
you hurled stones against the red clay
  they fell to a stream that sighed
accepted and washed
the wounds on the stones
for the sea

Ex-Proprietor

broken   stained
glass windows   barred
doors over which a grimy
Christ arms raised implores
the wrecker's ball to come soon
while waiting for the evening
light of
tenements

In Time

"the bedroom needs painting   it
needs curtains   what do you plan
to do about it"
    my answers don't satisfy
and wouldn't   the questions echo
through the house
hang near the ceiling
    in time the answers
will descend
perhaps as other questions

in bed two parallel bodies read
    though ready for sleep
i won't turn out my light first
it may shatter the fragile
silence

in the morning the ritual
of serving you coffee and grapefruit
in bed dispensed with
halfway out the door i thunder
"goodbye" twice   you rush
to an upper window and knock
    i glimpse your form and wave
our eyes don't meet

in time the answers
will come to us   together
or apart

For Beatrice

i laid you on the grass
beside a miser's house
   i kissed you knowing
it was something he
couldn't collect
   i kissed your white belly
and soft skin
where ivory is gold
the crumpled grass my envy
of the memory
i filled my pockets with

Memo for Toby

will you tell your father
before he goes
i heard the wild geese
flying north this morning
   he asked me last night
if i had

Frankly Christ

frankly Christ
i would rather someone else
remind us of our wound
   not the two thieves
they've been way up there
too long too
   rather any old man
accidentally cut
i delegate him to stain
the air   i want to know
that he is you

The Apartment

carefully dotted
i am lost
in my apartment
frantically tidying
   letters and books
in place
look particularly good
   i could
untangle the cords
of lamps close to their sockets
and straighten them into neat
circular piles   my heart
will not let me
   so i settle for a cigar
and let the smoke drift
through the window
where others are

Visitor

like sirens in the night
you came
   yet when i asked you
what was wrong
you had a coffee
and settled down
the old wound
still there

old friend
down and dripping
from a fight
you ask "what's tomorrow"
  as I bathe your wounds
i tell myself that tomorrow
like today may be
a book i buy
and your arm around
my shoulder

Neighbour

for Rose Tegano

woman bent almost full circle
with whom i shared the afternoon sun
the hands i've brought to bed tonight
are harsh   in prayer
they won't let me forget the earth
i kneaded for flowers
is prepared
for us

Lovers

why do we
the lovers after loving
walk as strangers
in the room

is it that love
the perfect Stranger
knocks
but never enters

For C.K.

i never returned
after you left
  i decided it should be
our place
and left it
at that

The Bell

there's a tiny bell
that moves about
   when it peals
it peals inside me
   each time it tolls
it's louder and
closer   oh
excuse me
there's the door bell

Ancient Chapel

here
by appointment
of artisan and
penitent

Fixture

for years
he was there every day
at the same time for
the same time

one day he didn't appear
gone for good it turned out
no one knew where
   though a few regulars
took long shots he'd been short
on words about himself   he'd kept
the conversation light despite
his eyes and receding frame

he was so quiet so much
a part of the place
none of us can describe him
enough to satisfy a stranger

he'll be missed   of anyone
we'd least expected him
to go

Woman of 35

i will go to sleep tonight
and sleep off years to come
  what else can i offer
to slow-forming wrinkles
that are gutters growing
for eternal rain

Travellers

on an Ottawa bus
she wanders back and forth
through the Canberra Times
want ads included
of 16 days ago
  fingers black from newsprint
fold the pages
of her thoughts
for safekeeping
  it stops for her
  eyes luminous
she disembarks
straightening
her hair

young chorister
elbow-guided in processional clasping
a taper that flickers
in your blind eyes   your voice
lights many rooms i've worn
blinders through
or flicked off lights in
to deny mirrors

Waiting

when i am drunk on Sundays
things like schoolbuses
take on humanity
because they are waiting

Petals

he leans into the tavern wall
   a cigarette
drops the occasional flower
on his overcoat lapel
   eventually he leaves
for fear of quarrelling
with the walls   the wind
devours the petals
driving ashes at him
and away

October

for Patsy

what more
you beside me
asleep in the October sun
while i with our daughter
talk among leaves
on their first
and final
wings

Morning Glory

last night cup frag
ments on the windowsill
   petals
this morning

To a Fanatic

take a walk
and come back
by yourself

Lunenburg

the thing i like
about draggers
is that they arrive
with such soft names
Sally   Susie   Daisy Mae
then cough up their lot of fish
and load
of wild men

Royal Navy Tradition

for Patsy

on shore
and vessels of quieter
waters breasts bare
for the returning
fleet   i see you
this way always
everywhere

Village Store, N.S.

every day
the old men shuffle here
where from nail kegs and rum
on the q.t. they dispose of
the world situation
with the authority of the ageless
cure-alls on the shelves
then shuffle back

Consistently Christian

every Sunday
packaged like Christmas
our neighbours present
their garbage

overnight
the autumn wind exposed
a nest i'd heard
though never seen

Zapata

though you were shot and killed Zapata
in the villages the word
passes from mouth to mouth
you are but hiding in the high sierra
and will return

in my country
i am reminded of you constantly
by the great river which for centuries
has been chanting your name
but cannot name you

Emiliano Zapata 1879-1919

Canadian Dialogue

your name is Susan
  yet for Madame Langlois
you signed your name
Suzanne

A Memory

you got on the bus
and again
when i got off
our eyes touched
   you are indelibly
January 28th 1987   not
what might have been
or might be   but
what is

Signposts

it's not the distances
that get to me
it's that the roads
are better marked than ever
  so many miles to there
the signposts say
  when i'm there
a few dead porcupines later
even if i turn back
it's so many miles again
  i want to arrive home
without warning

Diary Entries: Nov. 16 –

—NOBODY CAME TODAY
—NOBODY CAME today
—NOBODY came today
—nobody came today
—nobody came
—nobody
—no body
—no
    ”

my feet
my running feet
i cannot catch them